HARM'S WAY

First published in 2013
The Dedalus Press
13 Moyclare Road
Baldoyle
Dublin 13
Ireland

www.dedaluspress.com

ISBN 978 1 906614 62 1

Dedalus Press titles are represented in the UK by
Central Books, 99 Wallis Road, London E9 5LN
and in North America by Syracuse University Press, Inc.,
621 Skytop Road, Suite 110, Syracuse, New York 13244.

Cover image 'The Great Divide'
Oil on Canvas, 59 cm x 53 cm
by David Quinn
www.thefargarden.com

The Dedalus Press receives financial assistance from
The Arts Council / An Chomhairle Ealaíon

HARM'S WAY

Conor Carville

For Cliodhna
Feb. 2013

DEDALUS PRESS
DUBLIN, IRELAND

ACKNOWLEDGEMENTS

Acknowledgements are due to the editors of the following where a number of these poems or versions of them originally appeared:

'Minerva', 'Didymus', 'Gregg's Mill' and 'Oort's Cloud' were first published in *Poetry Ireland Review*. 'The Philosopher' and 'The Willow Pattern' were first published in *The London Magazine*. 'The Figures' appeared in *A Mutual Friend: Poems for Charles Dickens* (Two Rivers Press, 2012), edited by Peter Robinson.

For my Mother and Father

Contents

Touchdown

Thirteen hours on the redeye, the spell
as ever leaves the senses gloved,
half-asleep and yet eager to move,
following the pulse's boom to where a carousel

staggers into uneasy life, dislodging
your belongings, yours and those
of another: summer and winter clothes.
Who knows the kind of weather we'll be having.

Shiso

Hungry? A shiso leaf, its slick wedge
around a central cicatrice,
the teeth of each serrated edge
green against the white rice.

Broader at base, smaller,
it's something like a nettle leaf,
though of nettles I remember
mostly slim, baroque, canti-

levered leaves in layers, each one
a demesne of tiny spines,
each tip a dragon's mazy tongue.
So that can't be right.

Itadakimasu! I return to:
glistening muscle, seaweed
in strips, soy sauce to dilute
the shiso's dash of wasabi.

And away from those touchy crowds,
their crepuscular murmur,
how they seem to gain ground
when your back is turned.

Lupita

A cry from my bedroom wall at night,
as if someone were standing inside it,
a cross before and a cross behind,
like Saint Patrick's poor sister Lupita,

into whom, because of what she'd done
with Colman, the saint had put the fear
of Almighty God by calling on Odran,
his body-double and charioteer,

the original nutter, a spaceman,
to break out his couple of nags and to gun
his low-riding, customised wagon
over the courtyard's straw and dung

and into the Temple's half-finished interior.
The whole of the town was standing outside
that day, close enough to hear
how horseshoe and wheel-rim went silent

an instant, as if some fabulous creature's pelt
were lying on the dreaming parquet,
packed with honeycombs and fat
to crush around the steel and muffle it.

The whole of the town heard the clarion call
of voices raised, and one cut off,
like somebody with a snooker ball,
a pink or a red, crammed into their mouth,

so although they are screaming
nothing comes out, not a gasp
nor a gurgle, the ructions inside
lost to the world, as Lupita is lost

when the glistening ball, now sticky with sputum,
goes rolling unsteadily over the baize,
as the stone rolled away from the empty tomb
to Mary the Mother of God's amaze.

Patrol

Stowed away in the dark
of the half-collapsed loft,
you smoke and try not to cough
above the reek of Gallagher's byre,

plotting its realm
of extra-terrestial cairns
and keshes, alien drumlins
and smouldering freshets.

Into which they will pass,
the visitants, one by one,
the leader gently scoping the cows
and nodding the others on,

their webbed skulls laced
with leaves, padded with lichen,
their eyes locked in
beyond your spectrum.

Suspended animation.
I find myself turning to ice
as I watch the last of the silent line
step backwards into the milky night.

Ouija

At night the deep, invisible tugs
awaken even us, the heaviest of sleepers,
like whatever impels across the mirror
the glass that begins to touch and nudge,

now and now, the scraps of tracing paper,
hastily inked, that hover above the tain
and their own obscure reflections. If the stain
that deforms the tatty silver

seems to come between you and your image,
it doesn't, is rather embedded out here,
the lens of an unmanned camera
watching from its place beyond a language

torn and set adrift upon the patent surface.
Let's watch the papers flutter, their veering pass
in the wake of the shuttling glass
may let you do little but hastily parse

each disappearing word, each lithe phrase.
Yet elements, for all that, fall into place
and let us glimpse a world, a space
beyond the blur of flesh. And then it is erased.

Irish Dancing

The microphones embedded in our heels
ensure that punters in the final rows
of stadia are not forgotten. We wait for echoes,
but here they come alive with shrieks

and moans of feedback, distant calls
emerging from the dark, electrifying keens
convulsing the ballroom's primitive speakers.
It's as if an audience was held in thrall

already, though no one's there, not least
the legendary guy, somewhere to the rear,
we were taking for the sound engineer
of this rambling pile, lost above his frieze

of crysolite dials and obsidian buttons,
his veritable archive of chronic distortion.

The Wheelie-Bin

Monday mornings its gibber-flip
awakes me, the rough-and-tumble
of its drag against the cobbles
dislodging the greasy trap

of its gob, and as the flat head
is unhinged, so begins
the baffling ribbet, bringing
them up again, the dead

stogies and bits of string, the livid
slivers of plastic and peel
that spiral slowly to the street
before the lorry's gulp and fillet.

Flibbertigibbet. Comes back
empty but for the filth
that furs its gullet, the tilth
of swarf and milt impacted

to its floor, though not before
that tacky, flapping plastic bill
starts clacking even louder still,
battering out an afterword

that only just fails to make itself heard
above the whine and screech
of the dumper, a gallows speech
that is lost soon as uttered.

Starman

For twenty-nine years it's been evening,
the last of the day's heat clotting
silently in furrow and ditch.
A sticky finger flicks the switch
on a smuggled radio that all day
long has scored the news from Ballymurphy
with the shuffling triplets of Glam –
Tyrannosaurus Rex, The Sweet, also-rans
like *Mud.* And we've almost had our fill
of the ancient *Bhean a'ti,* her shrill
'Ná bí ag caint as Bearla!', so the blent
commotion swells and rises, our sole intent
to strip each berry from its row
before the Ulsterbus arrives to take us home.

But not before I catch a glimpse
of him, running as the sunset films
the back-drop of the hills,
and the crowd of our compadres dwindles
down to knots of blue and green:
my heart's desire, the Bowie clone
who has sat these three weeks past
like a cockatoo at the back of the class.
And now he stands before me, pale and calm,
and hanging off his slender arm
a plastic *C & A* bag weighed
with fruit, black and red
and purple spoils that have begun
to turn to jam already in the sun.

I watch as he begins to welt,
pell-mell, that sac of pulp
like a cellophane propeller,
cartwheeling it higher, harder, faster,
the androgenous face beginning to blur
above his cotton flares
and stripy V-neck combo;
and there's little I can do
to resist the powerful centrifuge
I'm slowly falling into,
till with a shift, an imperious twist,
of the sinews in his skinny wrist
the bag that mutters and hurtles round
is brought above the back-combed crown.

To what prospect might we have flown,
had the logo not split open
and flung in a glutinous arc,
over half the Donegal Gaeltacht
it seemed, that wedge of sticky goo?
It had the pines around us bruised:
dark-blue, blue-black. It had them contused.
Like the side of my face when I came to
in the deepest part of a dark driseog,
the Starman gone, his cover blown,
my hair a mass of tatters and dreads,
my skin awash in a *maquillage*
of jam in welts and gashes and wens,
red on my clothes and my face and my hands.

Top of the Pops: 1975

As soon as the gent from Ground Control
called Major Tom a second time
I thought: 'this isn't *Status Quo*', –
and the screen began to snow inside.

For a whiplash had paused in the window
above it, bisecting exactly the moon,
where the tail-end of a lost patrol
was tuning out our living room.

Retro

Picking her way through the slight seconds
she was convulsed by the language of clocks.
For days she ticked and stuttered,
hiccuping like a cracked CD,
and although we told her to pack it in,
she couldn't, never mind our BOO!s and *shhhhhhs;*
never mind holding her breath like a red balloon
or lapping the far lip of the cup.

The torture came to an end it is said
when she went back to the factory shop
and finally bought the rayon skirt
and the black plimsolls and the blue
neckerchief that reminded her so
of that Tippi Hedren in *Vertigo.*

Revision Session

Above the roof, transparently material,
something is up with the sky, something implied,
a covenant, a mechanical sign, alive
and in the same breath absent, invisible

now to those glancing up from grammar
or maths to see branches surge in the downdraught,
the all-weather pitch sanded and blasted
by that roiling din, the blades' hooped chatter.

Which will in its turn recede, a babel becoming
dimmer and dimmer, no more than the hum
that will serve, if memory serves, as backing track

to the rickety footage that sees us turn back
as a man to the class, back to the matter in hand,
away from the place where nothing has happened.

Excarnation

A horse-box, hearsed, in a copse.
I am looking for something to salvage.
Above the mudguard's pelmet
the wood is gummy with rot,
and as I work the housing clean
the whole near side begins to tear,
to come away, in a queasy dissolve
that takes back a life-time

in horse years. I have that image
still: the clatter of sixteen hands,
the greasy tarp of skin, the thunder-
head of flies released as I swoon,
pass out; and when I come to,
I'll find myself up to my neck in it.

The Takings

Tonight I'll force an entry
through the period detail
of that tiny fan-window.

After stashing the vinyl hold-all
that held now the evening's takings,
he started to silently freestyle.

It could have been '83 again,
so good was he still:
he popped and locked and body-rocked,

made angles of his bones until,
with one look towards me,
and one towards the ceiling,

he was suddenly gone, triggered
clean across the dancefloor.
The nip-and-tuck

of that back-flip
made angles of his bones
across the plate-glass windows,

while behind me his shadow
was thrown, thrown, thrown,
in the paddywagon's strobe.

The Tag

Melancholy of the fading tag,
silver and blue, narrowly there
as day begins to fold its flags
and banners. This close to the water

the streetlights' shivering paths,
become the Thames' familiars,
until the fog that wreathes
already the northern shore

has seen them fade from sight,
as the tag will fade in time,
and in that fading strike
more surely than what's left behind.

Field Recording

The sound engineer checked in last night
after months of miking-up kills,
skulking beneath a camouflaged hide
dug in on the plain, praying for jackals,

vultures to come and unveil
the gorgeous *musique concrète*
that scores their rending of deer and gazelle.
Worlds away from the Serengeti,

at the side of the cable-strewn lobby
he waits for the *tête-à-tête* to conclude
before the crew break up for coffee:
the tiny transmitter he'll deftly remove

from the breast of the Special Advisor
is speckled with blood, sheened with saliva.

The Bookshop

In the absence of some grand design
my hangover haunts the escalators,
the dumpbins, the islanded
tables landscaped with memoirs

and cookery. It ascends to the strip-
lit ceiling, a streal
of smoke beset with flickers,
grey against acres of taupe and teal.

Music filters through it: light opera.
Fleetwood Mac's *Rumours*.
The doors in here are like windows,
and the windows enormous

plasma screens, where Oxford Street's
industrial light and magic
incites the city's spectral spalpeens
to enact their flawed historical epic.

Flashdance. Toto and Moby.
My hangover hovers above the café,
caught up in a latte's
spiralling thermal; it stows away

in a virtually circular bagel's
perfectly virtual centre.
It has perched itself on the peg
of the cubicle door in the Gents'

tropical micro-climate
to watch as a shivering man
decants a hypodermic
gently into his throttled arm.

The Gypsy Kings. Dido. Ricky Martin.
A panpipe rendition
of 'Nights in White Satin'
that never – reaches – the end.

The Demonstration

The day that something happened to the gaze
had exhibitionists stripped to the waist

or halter-neck, as rapt voyeurs observed
the rituals of peek-a-boo and eye-swerve

under the gumshoe sun, panoptical.
Long before the demonstration's tail

had left the river it arrived, and all day
long the park filled up. From where I lay

the crowds metabolized, they emerged
and merged along pitch and verge,

while time went through one of its phases,
holding and breaking again like a wave.

By noon the gaze was holding up,
lean and bright, reflecting from a scrap

of metal hammered to a distant tree,
or moments later grazing a cheek,

skimming a thigh. In the smoky
glass of unmarked cars, in a telescopic

lens I caught it; it returned to me
from stud and piercing, visor and shield,

from the shiny laminate passes
of media men and security forces.

It shone through yellow plastic cordons.
It sparkled from the hats of traffic wardens.

Seen from the side of the eye,
as is often the case, the gaze seemed spry.

And yet these days, it's getting on.
For, after lunch, the alcohol all gone,

the speeches listened to, the book
stalls packed away, another look

crept in, a dull intensity that held its own
and nothing more. I turned for home,

and the gaze came too, it tagged along,
tired out by now, though I was strong

having paced myself for the homeward schlep.
Two of us then, retracing our steps

to the mouth of the park, as far as the Zoo,
where the gaze engaged in a short peruse

of the silky ocelli along the span
of a peacock's tinselled and tasselled fan,

and I thought for a moment 'All is well
with the world. The gaze has held'.

But no. Uh-uh. As the tail collapsed,
something faltered, something passed,

and a chopper turbined over us,
its stuttering blades repulsing

the sun, sieving it through their defiles
like fingers held over horrified eyes.

Fugue State

Up on the roof again tonight,
in arabesques that pelt and falter:
footsteps, drawing the line

above the room where I take shelter
in the usual state.
They pause and group. Scatter.

Fade. Yet when I awake
it's always into this nervous pall:
the silence on the fire escape

like the lull that follows landfall
on *Terra Nullis*. Come Four
there's activity in the peep-hole,

the top-floor landing's Mercator
distorting in its flawed geode.
My fragile poles: the flickering

low-wattage light; the blackened
foil on the communal walkway.
Now nothing comes between

me and the swarming stars
but the ceiling's chipboard
and lagging, the grimy spars

of concrete, the terrace
above them, fraught with fibre optics
and suckered with satellite dishes,

while in the hall, stirring stealthily,
lie the drifts of adverts and coupons
that scratch and patter in the breeze

like leaves or souls, bearing tales of fortune
and treasure-trove: *Pay-As-You-Go;*
All You Can Eat; We Never Close.

The Figures

Between Southwark Bridge which is made of silver
and London Bridge which is made of gold,
they float and hover, the figures, through-composed
by night and rain, rowing against the working river,
its writhing surface roped and plied
like a shadowy fosse of underground cables.

The earth turns and the body appears.
A camera too revolves, a leather barque
sets out once more towards the North, arch
that bends the starry dome. The whole sector
is on fire: oil, corn and copper at all-time highs
above All Hallows Lane and Angle Passage.

A second boat there. Even at this depth
I hear it graze and grate the other's stern
as one mouth says: 'What world does a dead man
belong to?' to which a second mouth
replies: 'The Other World'. 'And to what world
does money belong?' But here the currents

bear me off again: a glitch, a stitch, a chrysalis
slowly unspooling, whose data-cloud
of flags and flitters, whose wandering shroud,
seems but the more diaphanous
for the echo-graph of numbers and names
that stream around and through it, systemic change

cascading past the glassy cliffs,
the gates of silver and the gates of gold,
where passionate shadows trawl the cold

incessantly: stoking it with aching wrist,
stripping the *fattie wave* to the bone;
invisible hands that root in my cake-hole.

Found Poem

From Stith Thompson's *Motif-Index*
of Folk Literature (1932-37)

Man to meat.
Man to lard (Africa).
Man to feather (Tahiti)
Man to egg (Faroe islands)
Man to storm (Hottentot)
Man to wind (Hottentot)
Person to seafoam (Tuamotu)
Man to oceanwave (Tuamotu)
Man to fire. (India)
God to fire. (India)
Man to smoke (German)
Man to ashes (Hindu)
Man to ant-hill (Hindu)
Man to hair (Charpentier)
Man to spittle (Jewish)

The Phantom Limb

It quivered and then withdrew.
Back up it went,
recalled from our bedroom,
as if from an alien element

in which we were suspended,
breathless, staring up at the shoe-
shaped hole. The ceiling was rent
but we were conjoined below,

steeped only now in the innocent
moans of the afternoon's
traffic. This was The Elephant,
a fortnight after our move

to the top of the shabby tenement.
And as we lay in that ferrule
of light, our musty cerements
like Tutankhamun's

under Carter's torch, a descent
was expected, or the nominal view
of some haloed countenance
gazing through

the gap. But all was rapt and intent
up there, never a footstep flew
on the stairwell, no movement
stirred at all, save for a change in the hue

of the light, from moment
to moment, what light there was,
as it leaked into the apartment.
Only the very faintest of shadows.

An image
shines tonight out-
side, within

the window-
pane, it weaves
and trembles, a glow
riven from inside by waves

of blows, although it's the bass,
I'm guessing, from the car below
that sends a tremor through the glass
and makes me think it shudders so.

I shudder to think, am like the glass,
by turns alive then mineralized
as something beats outside
again: the passing bass,
the mirrored bulb's
effulgence.

Lodgings

If this room is breathing,
it is so gently,
you wouldn't believe,

so slowly,
that the woodchip plies,
subsides,

but doesn't tear.
The room comes alive,
but you'd be none the wiser,

till you put a mirror
in front of the mirror,
watch it mist and erase

only to mist again
in the self-same spot,
as the plumbing gives

that low-pitched, arthritic whistle,
and the window shudders,
loose in the frame

you have come this far to repair.

Die Familie Schneider

You will always remember the first house
drifting into the second, the same dead
air only different, dry and close,
a spoor of tangerines and fishheads

drifting into the second, the same dead
shadow persisting in washing away
the spoor of tangerines and fishheads,
that will remain nevertheless, will stay,

its shadow persisting. In washing away
at the unbreakable dish she holds
she too will nevertheless remain, will stay,
the centre of the scene that is unfolded.

The unbreakable dish she will hold
for the rest of her life, a life reduced
to the central scene that is unfolded,
watched from the hallway or the stairs

by the same impossible figure, the dead
same as her, only different. Dry and close,
he rustles, he whispers in the dark of her head:
'you will always remember the first house'.

At Seagahan

I skip across the cattle-grid, not caring how
each cylinder rings an octave
higher than its blank rebound,
how the notes congeal on contact

with the sky, how they quickly petrify
to skim across the reservoir,
a silver-blue acoustic dish that tries
to bounce each signal further

still, to route its progress clear
of the whole unnatural amphitheatre,
until they disappear like pings from sonar
when something huge returns to deeper waters.

Natural History

Supple woven shadow
of the moiré curtain: a waveform
moving on the floor beneath

the splintered casement.
Ripples shiver it, focal shift
as branches strain the light.

Across the road the new estate
is taking shape:
girders hum in the blue,

a distant glider takes the air
above the ornamental lake
and its crannóg of totalled cars.

Inside the porte-cochère
the clapper of an old alarm
rusts tightly to its crimson bell.

Our two abandoned bikes
tick in the long grass
at the edge of hearing.

The Birds

Paris looks bleached, eastern and hot
    from the Pompidou's roof,
though inside the tubular behemoth
    all is predictably cool

as we watch the impossible
    tangle of crows, effortless,
each working its angle,
    turning their taloned tails to us,

like those in the enormous still
    we saw here in the Hitchcock show:
the diving backs of crows and gulls,
    the human world on fire below.

Guests of the Nation

The tick of two clocks troubles
the air, a net of shadow trawls,
the saucepan gulps and bubbles
in the room beyond the wall.

The shallows of the small backyards
are sunk beneath the sky,
the planted fir trees in the park
shiver and swell behind.

The park and the pale cathedral
with its row of granite saints,
its double-jointed steeples,
all bleached and run with water stains.

And framed at the end of the narrow
hall that tunnels through the house,
a single open window's
emptiness looks out. Looks out

and in upon the scene
where figures talk and laugh,
yet dread the lifting of the dream,
for dreams will have their aftermath.

Gregg's Mill

In the silent house, in the watchful hall,
I am struck by shapes in the light that falls
to slick the shoulder, neck and cheek
of a figure coming from the fields.

I have turned into her abiding stare,
there's the detail of my mouth in hers,
held somehow, as if in amber:
she moves through me to the end of her tether.

Didymus

Between the Folly
and the Hole-in-the-Wall

a smoker's ghost
unlatched

the plastic
catch in her throat,

to blow me the ring
I wear still on my finger.

The Crane

They build themselves, you know,
working out at their own

edge, adding up to almost nothing:
a fretwork of white beams,

a skyhook; a tinted cab.
To come around in this drab

tower, becalmed in early light,
is often to find that, overnight,

another has joined the skyline.
Is to watch, between the blinds,

the crane begin the working day:
its desolate, infinitesimal sway

in a strong November breeze
that blows the mortar from the trees

like cinematic snow.
I have followed the long arm's slow

underwater swing, its weightless
gravity, its material grace

for days up here, parallel
with the cab, yet unable to tell

exactly where the cables end.
For the river sends

its mist across the site,
and I make do with second sight

and sound, straining to hear
the smooth revs, the ticking gears

as something rises from below,
steady as she goes,

and the white boom glides,
and the carriage on the underside

tracks across, to hold above its place
the dense, stained, invisible weight.

Hangman

1.

For every letter that you miss,
the pen is moved to make its stroke,
and build the gallows, so, its rope
snaking round to form a noose.

My mother introduced this game,
defusing backseat enmities
on late-night drives in the Seventies.
As we play I'm there again:

the wet forecourts, the reservoir,
white and blank, unruffled by rain,
the red car in the blue chicane
of planted pine, acre upon acre,

beyond which the sky glows, a ropeburn
meaning home. Though the checkpoints are gone,
and gone the gloved hands
that waved us through the towns

and villages, each terminal redoubt
obscuring its forerunner: Lisburn
and Lurgan, fair Portadown.
Craigavon's swings and roundabouts.

2.

I watch, high above Heathrow,
you stare in mute opprobrium
across the aisle, as mum
and daughter conjure rope and hollow

head, neck and crooked tree, then spell
them out again, a dozen per sheet,
and imagine that I see
your reading of this *gaijin* ritual,

the half-erected scaffolding
over each completed word
emblematic of a culture long inured
to the half-known thing, half told.

How this will make you long again
for Kanji, Hiragana, Katakana
and all the delicate arcana
in which you are instructing me in vain.

The rest of the flight is spent at sea,
drawing hangmen, row upon row
above the words you won't disclose.
When we touch down I take them with me.

3.

The airport is empty, and, save for
the air-conditioner's steely breeze,
an oven. My father is asleep beneath
the enormous digital billboard

where pixilated archipelagoes
degrade themselves, minute by minute,
slowly adopting the format
of the same old execrable logos:

BP; AOL; HSBC.
In minutes we are on the road,
and in seconds childhood
overtakes me. Unable to speak

I mouth the ancient acronyms
visible still on the Armagh Road,
the overwritten binary codes
of one and zero sums,

while you stay silent in the back,
and the motorway bridges short
the latest local news reports,
strafing the signal with blanks.

4.

How to explain the importance
of what little we're prepared
to tell? Remember your despair
at my struggle for the sense

of those fifteen standing stones
in the temple at Ryoanji,
each arranged so skilfully
that one was lost wherever we'd go?

Just lately I have caught their drift:
that bountiful subtraction
as every stone in turn is hidden.
And each of us an interstice.

You've no more need to second-guess
these consonants and vowels,
than I to add another gallows
to the world. Let our enduring crest

be one no heraldry commands;
for what survives
is incomplete and we
are happiest that almost understand.

Two Cranes

They work as a pair, very close,
but alone, each disclosed

beyond the others' orbital
and within their own: a sentinel

overlooking its patch.
And if they seem to overlap

that's not the case at all,
but rather where you sit, the angle

you are watching from, day in,
day out. For if they did those lines

would snag and tangle, the booms
would fail, as would their dream-

like dance of pass and counter-
pass, of skyhooks raised and lowered –

decorous and artificial
as any courtship ritual.

No. They negotiate at distances,
and miss each other by inches,

preserving in that gap, that play
of space, the necessity of giving way

and therefore holding fast.
Often when we pass

at night, on reaching the corner
one of us will stop the other

below them, parallel against the sky:
not quite touching; perfectly aligned.

Kuzunoha

'Come in, Conor-*san*. Leave that alone.
Tomorrow it will still be there.
Its not going to anywhere'.
I trap this poem beneath a pine-cone,

it's every scale so tightly sheathed
by the one next-door, you couldn't scry
an edge between them, and pass inside
to where the flow of speech

is broken, now and then, by a snicker
like that of a fox. Turning in, I hear
the wary tap of the cistern, the whimper
and bump of the ancient boiler:

they go right through me, till
I shell into my ears the tiny cones
she aggregates from home-
bound flights, and through them fall

asleep. Later, I'll leave another room,
stepping backwards through,
and through, construe
a smooth systole as paper-thin

partitions gliding in their grooves.
That have no sooner closed
than I am shown
their other, farther side infused

with ink, the signs appearing
as if from nowhere, as if written in
the air I breathe. And for that instant
I can read: 'If you still love me, dear

then search me out beneath the pines
of Shinoda forest in Izumi,
where those shivering trees
cast upon my back their rain of tines'.

Failing to Climb Fuji

We could count these steps forever,
moving two abreast and whispering aloud,
and doubling back on ourselves from level
to level until, reaching the top, we'd avow

together the total that we'd climbed.
But in truth the numbers will fail to tally
and, looking down, one of us will find
the missing step we'd long heard tell of

missing once again, its faint subtraction
caught like a breath between one word, one
thought, one continent and another.

So let's just sit in silence here, turning
round and about in our heads once more
the perfect volcano's invisible core.

Continental Philosophers as TV Detectives

"In times of terror, when everyone is something of a conspirator,
everyone will be in a situation where he has to play detective,"
—Walter Benjamin, *The Paris of the Second Empire in Baudelaire.*

If Foucault is Kojak, and Felix and Gilles
are Starsky and Hutch, then you, Walter,
are looking at Columbo, which is no bad deal,
not bad at all, though the grizzled possessor

of the shonkiest raincoat in Los Angeles
might seem like a no-mark, the kind of sucker
you find in titty bars, he knows his own field
backwards, like you and your rival Heidegger,

who is of course Ironside, the eminence gris,
grafting his way through enforced retirement,
brooding on Mr Big (the B uppercase, as in Being)
while scooting around in his wooden bunker

below the Police Department. Columbo isn't keen.
It's a gimmick he thinks, the wheelchair,
camouflage for the mage routine. There's no need
for staginess: the chiaroscuro Raymond Burr

emerging from the darkness shtick is feeble.
Better to polish the back of your pompadour
with your dented gabardine's greasy sleeve,
ratchet your forehead and sidle back and forth

committing the décor to memory: the Nietzsche
bust, the dinky alpine shepherdess cavorting
on the counterpane, the Grinch himself, wreathed
in stoic silence, regarding the curious visitor

who signs the leather day book, then heaps
a hundred pages in his hand to let them pour
back through decades of prime-time, carefully
noting the names, how the slipway of each signature

gathers into the twentieth century's
demented spaghetti junction, its three or four
or five combobulated switchbacks, each one an allegory
for another, the past doing time for the future,

the future reaming the past, while the present recedes
in the rear-view mirror of an odd French car,
grubbily battered, packed with newspapers and candy
wraps, index cards and Bonaparte cigars.

Yes, it's you again, cruising slowly out to Irvine,
explaining *Galassenheit* to your dog, a dour
and nameless basset hound from central casting,
whose sorrowful gaze you've internalized

and cannot unlearn. It's the final episode, season six:
'The One that Got Away'. At the top of the hour,
we see the activating incident, a messy domestic
somewhere near Laguna, where a visiting professor

comes round from a series of mental events
to see, peeking from between her teeth,
the awful frozen popsicle of his dead wife's tongue.
And so the inverted format unwinds, the anti-

plot where all is revealed at the start of the show,
and we shamble backwards towards it, so that guilt or
intention are never at issue, and we know
in advance where the bodies are buried. All except yours.

The vanishing point. The future you fell through
all of your life. From Berlin, Moscow, Paris to Port Bou,
where a figure lights up in a darkened hotel room,
his neck-tie unshackled, his felt hat a gumshoe's.

The Philosopher

I know there is blackness and whiteness in snow,
for how otherwise could the winter sun
make the water run dark through Athenian gardens?
O the animal senses are fine, as far as they go,

but miss the point of the point in time
where flesh conjoins with wheat, wheat with gold,
meteors with eclipses, sandstorms with rainbows.
You people are better off studying the sky

than a goat's turd, but don't look for omens.
Imagine instead a Scythian's blanket
unrolled in our agora, his astral trinkets
thawing into the soft blue felt: adornments

for the barbarian ear, winking coins, crystal
spear-tips. This shining diadem of pine cones
stolen from the Persian court was once,
like the sun, a boiling mass of many kinds of metal.

That's the only kind of provenance worth pursuing.
Forget about stamps or papers, leave that to the men
who ask me if I think about my native land.
To whom I answer, 'why of course I do!'

gazing upwards, pointing to the stars.

Kandinsky Among the Komi

You tell me the stars are nailed to the sky,
and I recall the copper tacks
that tamp the empty canvas
to its stretcher. Who am I to say the drive

that hammers each one softly home
does not secure the night, pliable and taut,
an oval drum above the steppe
and the singing taiga where the Komi

stitch images of loons and crosses
to their hems and their cuffs and their collars?
Your reindeer coat mislays its halo
more than once, and sometimes antlers

rise above your head in my pictures.
Lost in conversation with the fire,
you thoughtfully undress, as I conspire
to sketch your irregular features.

Calenture

The tell-tale symphony of creaks and moans
came into our heads again today,
the whole superstructure in play
around us: the rigging's tautened strum
in the trees, and beneath the road
invisible trains like shifting cargo.

Before us the city's skeleton crew
began to assemble itself, the mate's
resigned, implacable gaze in each passing face
took root, and at length a tattoo –
that eye you remember the captain
had – crawled again in the palm of my hand.

Those sounds once more: Greene Street's *mêlée*
ship-shaped into new permutations.
But if the pile-driver's patient
boom resembles the crash of a heavy swell,
if shutters collapse with the shearing of canvas,
it's from such sounds that dreams preserve us.

Yet back they come. And we are given to know
that this shop-front, the pavement below,
the book in your hand,
your very hand itself, though
they seem of the city, of the hard dry land,
are this day lost at sea. The sea is not calm.

Woodworm

Riddle of pores, anti-braille,
unreadable merely
as symptom or outcome,

and if not world in itself
then a way of the world,
each larval harrowing

a patient, silent
invisible graft
that works for years

beneath the thinnest
of veneers before the sudden
emergence. How deep,

you ask, do they go,
these careful burrows? Well,
How long have you got?

As your capillaries,
unraveled, might reach
to the moon and back.

so the galleries inside
this single chest
laid end to end

could girdle the earth,
the four-square box so hollowed
a single glance could overturn it.

Torus

On the last day, so Origen writes, we'll all
become spheres and roll into heaven:
pure surface, all hollow and ringing, no end
nor beginning. One and nil.

You can see the attraction. But the sphere
concept has problems surely? So sure
of itself, the sphere, so endlessly
plumbed by its own centrality.

Let's moot another shape, vast
and lightly-frosted, rotating through the outer
reaches of the universe: a doughnut,
holed up somewhere beyond its own sweet matter.

The Observatory

1.

It has never ceased to resound,
a sonic wall, dense as Spector's
that topples slowly and forever
forward. Nothing turns it down,

it has the universe surrounded,
yet he must take its measure
still, plot a true course
against the darkness of its ground.

2.

The white machines that never give in
are dreaming in numbers.
To each screen its yellow tablet, a rapid blur
of digits relayed from a mountain

umpteen zones away. The dead volcano glows.
Night falls. The circular
rigs grill the crystalline air.
Long after he has left for home

and the bedroom where he moans
and shivers, listening for
his own heart murmur,
the figures flee on in the dark, are combed.

through matrices, translated into sound,
the tremor that will score
his coming days, the Ur-roar
he drowns out with talking books and Motown.

The Willow Pattern

Above and beyond the bridge, the willow,
a pair of doves like tattooed swallows

contorting on a sailor's breast, evidence that land
is near, inky and indelible, sign of safe return.

Or blurring into the back of my fist, proof
of the time when I could handle myself

and was damned for it: the china from Kiangsi
squeaking in the spicy dark, holding high and dry

the tea, its weight transfixing stars and spiders
to the uppermost tiers, though underwater

in the bilge, a massive reef of plates survived.
For weeks the columns tottered on the dockside,

and fell, as fall they did, with the cataractic roar
of a slaver's chandelier I saw tipped overboard

an age ago in Saint Domingo. The cheer that flared
along the splintered quays was loud enough, I swear,

to wake the millions of Atlantic dead.
At night I heard them shoal against the bulkhead:

pale maroons and keening coolies, teagues
and tars and lascars, that legion of the underdog

whose nation is the sea. The want of opium
it was vouchsafed such visions –

our swaying tree of liberty, our mystic rose
that love nor war nor wisdom overthrows.

Now my soot-smeared clock beats out of time,
and the moon-lit fire sprouts secret flames

that play upon your dowry gift, this plate of chinaware.
Though English-made, from English bone and earth,

its willow branches squirm across the porcelain
like the giant centipedes of Port-of-Spain,

the creeping junk reminds me of Shanghai,
the wall of smoke that screens me from your eyes

resolves into the wall that separates the lovers.
And yet cannot, for all is simultaneous here

where fear and flight occur at once, the details volatile
like lives, shifting place and shape and scale

to circumscribe the sphere: clouds, currencies,
liquid as the fortunes of the Company

that conjures opium from indigo, human flesh from sugar
the way a god might change a man and wife to birds.

Sherry's Fields

It saws the air, a corrugated sound,
cardboard ripping along its seams,
as I break the Amazon boxes down
and notice the railings, rusty

where they were wrenched apart
by some neighbourhood legend
so that, it is said, a boy could dart
from out of the path of the Saracens

and into the green, municipal fields,
where a flapping, tattered, collapsible cross
would take him down the sixty degrees
of the bank of sun-yellowed grass

that is visible from our window still,
take him down to the couple
of courts where Mârek, and other locals,
are experimenting with mixed doubles.

The Flight Path

for Alannah

Each spiraling howl no sooner abates
than another one starts up, the bedroom's
cauldron roiled, thickened, hammered upon
an hour before daybreak. You speculate,
test the air, querulous before you scare,
then join your voice to the choiring turbines

that are louder by now, and closer together,
the big beasts from Boston and Hong Kong,
disengaging the stacks to prowl along
the perishing river, black as a bin-liner,
shook out past Bermondsey and Bankside
to St. Thomas's, where your unearthly cry

was struck up first amidst the warp and weft
of pattering data, the sinuous sighs
of Gas & Air, the polyglot chat of the midwives.
At six the doctor came and by her leave we left,
reaching home at dawn to hear the drone
set up again, glimpse an underbelly pass, wan

between the clouds, imagine droplets streaming
from its fuselage, the shuddering wings
taking on the light that escaped us still.
But as the sun came up the skies went silent,
for pressures fluctuate, fronts come from nowhere,
and at a single impulse from the tower

the whole grid can wheel around the city, all
the traffic of the air, all the souls who sleep,
their faces fiery in the screens that keep
the flight-path's distance, channeled by the new control,
so we wake up to nothing more than your small sounds,
while the engines start to clamour on the other side of town.

Minerva

Multiply, divide,
join the dots of the I

to this, to that.
To the multiple fly-

past of swifts,
to Warrenpoint,

to Poyntzpass.
To all points

in between us.
To a country road

with its empty sounds:
hooplah

of cuckoo, the dove's
pow-wow,

and the man laying low
in cahoots with the owl

who is wearing his head
the other way round.